Discipleship
the journey of faith

NICK FAWCETT

First published in 2002 by
KEVIN MAYHEW LTD
Buxhall, Stowmarket, Suffolk IP14 3BW
Email: info@kevinmayhewltd.com

9 8 7 6 5 4 3 2 1 0

ISBN 1 84003 921 3
Catalogue No 1500513

Cover design by Angela Selfe
Edited by Katherine Laidler
Typesetting by Louise Selfe

Printed and bound in Great Britain

Contents

To the ministers and clergy with whom
it was such a pleasure to work during my time
as minister of Gas Green Baptist Church, Cheltenham

Acknowledgements

The publishers wish to express their thanks to Cambridge University Press, The Edinburgh Building, Shaftesbury Road, Cambridge, CB2 2RU, for permission to reproduce the extract from The Book of Common Prayer (adapted), the rights in which are vested in the Crown.

Bible quotations are taken from the New Revised Standard Version of the Bible, copyright © 1989 by the Division of Christian Education of the National Council of the Churches of Christ in the USA. Used by permission. All rights reserved.

Introduction

Standing beside the little chapel on the windswept cliff top, it was hard to believe this remote spot on the western tip of Wales was once a centre of pilgrimage, a place to which Christians, across the centuries, made their way to pray, reflect and seek spiritual blessing. The only 'pilgrims' there that day were backpackers and holidaymakers.

In some traditions, of course, pilgrimage is still very much alive, shrines such as Lourdes attracting people in their thousands. Other traditions are less enthusiastic, even hostile to the idea. In a sense, however, we are all pilgrims, or at least we should be, for every one of us is called to follow the way of Christ. As John Bunyan recognised centuries ago in his religious classic *Pilgrim's Progress*, faith is about a journey as well as a destination, the path of discipleship calling for perseverance, trust and courage. As we will explore further in this book, becoming a Christian is not an end in itself but the start of a lifetime's pilgrimage. We are those who travel towards the city of God, who look forward to a new heaven and a new earth in which the old will have passed away. This is the vision that inspires our pilgrimage, the goal towards which we strive, but if the destination is important the journey is equally so. In this life at least, we never reach a point where we can stop and take our ease. On the contrary, to be true to itself, faith must always be growing, ready to explore ever-new horizons.

I have not focused in these studies on the end of the journey – that must wait for another book. Rather, I have concentrated on the journey itself. Where does it start? How does it affect us? What should we take for it? What does it entail? Can we finish it? Whom can we turn to along the way? In short, are we committed to a pilgrimage, or has faith become stuck in a rut, no longer the great adventure it seemed when we first set out? To return to John Bunyan, his great hymn encapsulates the challenge:

Who would true valour see,
    let him come hither;

one here will constant be,
    come wind, come weather.
There's no discouragement
shall make him once relent
his first avowed intent
    to be a pilgrim.

Is that our testimony? We may have sung the words many times, but do we mean them? God has called us to journey in the footsteps of Christ? Are we ready to follow?

Nick Fawcett

Leader's notes

I suggest using the material in this book as follows:

- Each session begins with a traditional prayer, followed by a short paragraph introducing the overall theme. It is worth reading this aloud, to set the scene for the session.

- After this I have included 'Activity' sessions, designed to break the ice and to encourage informal reflection on the theme of the study. Allow ten minutes or so for these, but do not allow them to dominate the session.

- Next comes a Bible passage (my own paraphrase unless otherwise stated). This should be read aloud, and then time given for group members to quietly ponder its meaning.

- Ideally, group members need to have read the 'Comment' section before the meeting, in which case you will need to have circulated booklets in advance of the first session. Alternatively, extend the period of quiet after the reading so that participants can read this section at their own pace.

- The 'Summary' section highlights the key points of the Comment. The leader should read this aloud before inviting people's thoughts on the subject so far.

- Allow discussion to develop and introduce as appropriate the questions provided in the Discussion section. It may be appropriate at this point to bring in the passage suggested for further reading, though you may prefer to leave this, as I have done, to round off the theme nearer the end.

- Pause for prayer, using the prayer provided, a prayer of your own, or a time of quiet/open prayer.

- After allowing ample time for discussion, read the meditation to draw people's thoughts together. The meditations in weeks 2 and 3 have been written specially for this book; the others are taken from my earlier publications *No Ordinary Man* and *The Unfolding Story*.

- Briefly, outline the suggestions for action. Invite any further ideas from among the group. From the second week onwards, you might also give people the opportunity to share how they applied the suggestions from the previous week.
- Finally, end the meeting in prayer, using either the prayer provided or your own.

Prayer

Loving God,
    you call us to a journey of faith,
    but sometimes that journey grinds to a halt.
We get stuck in a rut,
    closed to new directions,
    bogged down by the past,
    or reluctant to step into an unfamiliar future,
    preferring the view we know
    to horizons that might stretch and challenge us.
Move within us through your Holy Spirit,
    meet with us through the risen Christ,
    and so give light to our path
    that we may step forward in faith,
    and travel onwards wherever you might lead,
    through Jesus Christ our Lord.
Amen.

First week

Called to a journey

Opening prayer

O Lord Jesus Christ,
  who is the way, the truth, and the life,
  suffer us not to stray from you, who is the way,
  nor to distrust you, who is the truth,
  nor to rest in any other thing than you, who is the life.
Teach us, by your Holy Spirit,
  what to believe,
  what to do,
  and in what to take our rest.
Amen.

Erasmus

Introduction

When did you first become a Christian? Some people will answer a question like that without a moment's hesitation, naming the year, month and even day when they first made a public commitment to Christ. Others will find the question difficult if not impossible to answer, for them commitment having developed over a period of time or seeming always to have been part of their lives. Is the question, though, a fair one? Personally, I've always been uneasy with the phrase 'to become a Christian'. I know what it means and why it is said, but it gives the impression we are talking about a one-off event, a single action that, in a flash, takes us from one state to another. In a sense, of course, that is perfectly true, commitment to Christ marking a fresh chapter in our lives in which, by God's Spirit, we are born again, becoming a new creation. Yet that is only half the story, and the danger is that through emphasising this aspect, the other half never comes to be written.

Let me illustrate the point. I like to think of myself as a supporter of Southend United Football Club. In my mid- to late-teens I watched them play most weeks, my home being just a couple of minutes' walk from the ground and, although I moved away from the town 25 years ago, I still keep track of the team's fortunes, hoping that one day things might take a turn for the better. Indeed, I have even taken to looking up the club's official website to catch the latest match report or news. Sadly, though, I haven't watched the team play for over ten years, and that, I'm afraid, exposes the true nature of my 'support'. I may be interested in the team, but I can no longer claim to be a follower, for that requires continued action on my part. Unless I am there on the terraces, cheering on the players, contributing to the club's finances through paying at the turnstiles, my support is nominal, more illusory than real.

The parallel between this and nominal discipleship is not hard to spot. Many of us claim to be Christians, but when was the last time we darkened the door of a church, turned the pages of a Bible, approached God in prayer, or expressed our faith through practical service? Nominal discipleship, however, is not the only danger. We may consider ourselves followers of Christ, having made an act of commitment. We may even be part of a local church, actively involved in its affairs, yet, in terms of Christian discipleship, simply be treading water, no longer looking to grow in faith or expecting fresh challenges. A public act of commitment is necessary for us all, whether it involves a dramatic experience of conversion or a gradual coming to faith, but that is not the end of the matter. As far as I am aware, Jesus never suggested becoming a Christian involves a one-off decision, or that once we are a Christian we're always a Christian! Quite the contrary: conversion, whether sudden or gradual, is only the first step in a continuing pilgrimage. In that sense, we do not become but are constantly becoming Christians as, together, we walk the way of Christ.

Activity

Journeys quiz (see page 72).

Reading: Genesis 12:1-5; Mark 1:16-20; Matthew 9:9

The Lord said to Abram, 'Leave your country, your kinfolk and your father's house and head for a land that I will show you. I will make a great nation of you. I will bless you, and make your name celebrated, so that you will be a blessing. I will bless those who bless you, and curse whoever curses you; and through you all the families of the earth shall be blessed in turn.' So Abram, along with Lot, set off, as the Lord had told him, taking his wife Sarai, his nephew Lot, the various possessions they had accumulated, and the servants they had acquired while in Haran. At the age of seventy-five, he set off with them to go to the land of Canaan . . . As Jesus passed along the Sea of Galilee, he saw Simon and his brother Andrew casting a net into the sea – for they were fishermen. And Jesus said to them, 'Follow me and I will make you fish for people.' And immediately they left their nets and followed him. As he went a little farther, he saw James son of Zebedee and his brother John, who were in their boat mending the nets. Immediately he called them; and they left their father Zebedee in the boat with the hired men and followed him. As he was walking along, he saw a man called Matthew sitting at the tax booth; and he said to him, 'Follow me.' And he got up and followed him. (NRSV)

Comment

How would you respond if someone asked you what it means to be a Christian? Would you answer in terms of doctrine, spelling out the things a Christian needs to believe? Would you talk about baptism, confirmation or Church membership, stressing the need for personal conversion and public testimony to newfound faith?

Or would you perhaps emphasise that the way we live and the things we do are as important as the things we say, if not more so? As with most questions, there are various answers we could give, each capturing part but not all of the truth, but one, I believe, takes us nearer than any other: the nickname, 'followers of the Way'. That epithet, applied originally to members of the early Church, reminds us that faith is a way of life rather than a one-off act of commitment. Not that any of us would consciously want to separate the two, yet sometimes we can forget the fact that faith is a journey as much as a destination, a walking with God in an unfolding pilgrimage.

Nobody exemplifies that better than Abraham, or Abram as he was initially known. Comfortably settled in Haran, he suddenly felt the urge to move on, an urge that he came to recognise as the call of God. In a sense, this was Abram's moment of 'conversion', in that a new level of commitment was asked of him, a decisive response to God's summons, but the call was not to a statement of belief but to a journey of faith. It is hard to overemphasise the enormity of what this involved. This wasn't a brief trip down the road to a land paved with milk and honey. It wasn't 'Consult your atlas, and go to such and such a place, map reference XY'. He could offer no forwarding address to his friends or even any idea where he might end up. There was no knowing what the journey might involve, where it might lead or how long it might take. The future was in God's hands rather than his own. As the book of Hebrews puts it, 'By faith Abraham obeyed when he was called to set out for a place that he was to receive as an inheritance; and he set out, not knowing where he was going' (11:8, *NRSV*).

Was Abraham to settle again? In a sense, yes, and in a sense, no, for though he was to reach the land God had promised, life from then on was to take the form of a nomadic existence, travelling from place to place, open to new horizons and possibilities, to wherever God might lead him. In the words of Hebrews once more, '[H]e looked forward to the city that has foundations, whose architect and builder is God' (Hebrews 11:10, *NRSV*). The visible journey of Abraham's life was matched by an inner one: a walking with God, growing and maturing in faith, learning to trust despite appearances and recognising that the future is in God's hands. Having left the land of Haran, life for Abraham was never to be the same again; he had set out on the pilgrimage of a lifetime.

So it was too for those Jesus called as his disciples. All of them faced a decisive moment, a challenge to respond and commit themselves in faith, but far from being the end of discipleship it was only the first step on a continuing journey. To each came the same call, 'Follow me' – first Simon Peter and Andrew, then James and John, then Levi (or Matthew, as he became known), and so it was to go on throughout his ministry. To the rich man who came asking what he must do to inherit eternal life, he gave the answer, 'Go, sell what you own, and give the money to the poor, and you will have treasure in heaven; then come, follow me' (Mark 10:21b, NRSV). And to all those considering the call to discipleship: 'If any want to become my followers, let them deny themselves and take up their cross and follow me' (Mark 8:34b, NRSV). For the disciples, or at least for Peter as their spokesman, a confession of faith was to come later as understanding dawned, but that too was just one more step in a continuing journey. The challenge was not just to believe but also to act, not simply to hear the gospel but also to put it into practice, not merely to accept but also to follow.

Do *we* still have that perspective on faith? Do we still see ourselves as being involved in an ongoing journey of discipleship, or have we fallen into the trap of thinking we've made our commitment, done all that needs doing? 'I am the way, and the truth, and the life', said Jesus (John 14:6, NRSV), and that effectively says it all. We are followers of the way, a travelling people called to a lifetime's pilgrimage, and if we lose sight of that need to continue moving forward, seeing faith instead as a state we have reached, a destination in itself, then we will have become Christians in name only.

Have we committed ourselves to Christ? If so, well and good, we've made a start, but don't mistake the beginning for the end. More important, have we committed ourselves to following him, to walking his way and following the journey through?

Summary

- Being a Christian is more than simply declaring our faith or believing in God. It is more also than having experienced conversion or made a public act of commitment. Above all, it is about journeying in faith.
- For Abram, later to become Abraham, that involved a literal journey, tearing up his roots and living as a nomad as he travelled from place to place for the rest of his life. This journey was mirrored by an inward journey, his faith growing and maturing throughout his life.
- For the disciples, faith involved following Jesus. As with Abraham, they committed themselves to a journey from which there would be no going back.
- Do we still see ourselves as being involved in a lifetime's pilgrimage, or do we feel we have made our commitment and can now let faith take care of itself? Do we still have a sense of moving forward in faith?
- We may have made the first step in discipleship, but are we committed to seeing our journey through to its end?

Discussion

- Do you think we can lay too much emphasis on a single moment of conversion? What dangers are involved in this? Conversely, can we underplay the need for conversion?
- What do you see as involved in following Jesus? In what ways can we and should we follow him?
- What can cause us to lose sight of faith as a journey?

Prayer

Lord Jesus Christ,
    you call us, as you called your first disciples, to follow you:
    not simply to believe,
    to declare our faith and confess you as Lord,
    but to keep on following wherever you lead.
Help us to do that faithfully,
    pursuing the way of love and accepting the road of sacrifice.
Open our eyes to the great adventure of faith
    and to the unfathomable mysteries of your purpose,
    and so help us to live as pilgrims,
    travelling together in faith.
Teach us what it means to be a disciple,
    and, by your grace, help us to respond
    and to be followers of your way,
    to the glory of your name.
Amen.

Meditation of Peter

He called me to follow,
    to lay down my nets and follow him.
No time to think,
    to weigh up the pros and cons;
    then and there, the need to decide.
So I did,
    on the spot –
    left everything to become one of his disciples.
And I'm glad.
No, honestly, despite everything, I'm glad,
    for I know it was the right decision,
    the only decision I could have made.
Yet if I'd known then what I know now
    it might all have been very different.

I'd have thought twice, that's for certain –
    made sure I understood the small print –
    and very likely I'd have got cold feet.
You see, I'd no real idea what I was taking on,
    even though I thought I had.
I imagined he wanted me for a few days,
    a few weeks at most,
    and then, having done my bit, I could return home,
    back to friends and family,
    back to the security of my fishing nets,
    back to the way things had always been –
    but he soon put me right on that, didn't he?
He made it quite clear that discipleship is a lifelong commitment,
    not an option you can walk away from as the mood takes you.
Well, a few of us soon considered chucking it in,
    cutting our losses before we got in too deep.
Only we couldn't do that,
    not when it came to it,
    for we knew though he was asking much, he was offering more.
He had the answers we were looking for,
    the words of eternal life,
    and to have walked away then
    would have been to turn our backs
    on our one true chance of happiness.
So we carried on,
    day after day,
    week after week,
    month after month,
    following in his footsteps,
    sharing in his work.
And it was tough going, I can tell you,
    really tough –
    believe me, as a fisherman I know what I'm talking about.
Yet somehow we always found the strength we needed,
    just as he said we would,
    or at least we did until that awful last week

when suddenly it all went wrong –
the week Judas betrayed him, the soldiers arrested him,
and Pilate condemned him;
the week when we all ran for our lives,
our love and loyalty forgotten.
It was terrible,
more dreadful than my worst nightmares –
I've never known fear or sorrow like I felt then,
and I asked myself as never before,
'Why did I ever get mixed up with Jesus?'
I still ask that sometimes, more often than you might imagine,
for it's not got any easier following him.
There've been sacrifices to make,
suffering to endure, rejection to face,
and I know that one day, unless I'm much mistaken,
I shall pay the ultimate price.
So yes, if I'd known then what I know now
I might have decided differently.
It's possible – I really don't know –
but I'm glad I didn't,
for though it's been difficult and invariably demanding,
it's been wonderful also,
and I know not only was it the right decision,
it was the best I could ever have made.

Further reading: John 12:26

Whoever serves me must follow me, and where I am, there will my servant be also. Whoever serves me, the Father will honour. (*NRSV*)

Suggestions for action

Reflect further on what it means to travel in faith and consider how far you are still doing that. Commit yourself once more to the journey of discipleship.

Closing prayer

Lord Jesus Christ,
 teach me not just to acknowledge you as Lord,
 but to follow you in faith,
 and to walk wherever you would lead,
 to the glory of your name.
Amen.

Second week

A personal journey

Opening prayer

O Holy Spirit of God,
    take me as your disciple;
    guide me, enlighten me, sanctify me.
Control my hands that they may do no evil,
    cover my eyes so that they may see it no more,
    and sanctify my heart so that evil may not dwell within me.
Be my God; be my guide.
Wherever you lead I will go;
    whatever you forbid I will renounce;
    and whatever you command me,
    in your strength I will do.
Lead me, then, into the fullness of your truth.
Amen.

Henry E. Manning

Introduction

There's no substitute for experience, we sometimes say, and few would want to deny that. Although we can put ourselves in others' shoes to a certain extent, we cannot fully empathise with their situation unless we have been through it ourselves. If I were to write about life as a Baptist minister, for example, I would know what I was talking about, for I spent many years being just that, but if I attempted to write about life as an Anglican vicar or Roman Catholic priest, it would be a different matter. I would have to check my facts, read up on these two traditions, talk to representative clergy and so on, and even then my writing would almost certainly contain inconsistencies. Instead of detailing my own experience, I would be documenting that of others, and something would inevitably be lacking. Equally important, if not more so, first-hand experience engenders understanding in a way that borrowed experience cannot begin to. We might read a book, for example, on how to conduct open-heart surgery or fly an aeroplane, but that doesn't mean we could do those. Even if we had the theory at our fingertips, putting it into practice would be an altogether different proposition. It is not for nothing that we speak of learning in the university of life. Until we experience something for ourselves, it is not really part of us.

So it is in the journey of discipleship. Although we can overplay the experience of conversion or public commitment, such moments are nonetheless vital, for they testify to faith having become *ours*; no longer a matter of what we have learned as children or been told by others, but a living, daily experience. The process by which that happens may be sudden or gradual, but unless faith at some point involves a personal response it will not be faith at all. Not only must the response be personal, however; so too must the journey. Your experiences of faith will not necessarily be the same as mine; indeed, every person's will be different, for God deals with us not as part of a nameless crowd but as individuals. We cannot borrow from someone else's journey; we have to pursue our own. That is what it means to walk the way of Christ.

Activity

Personal journeys quiz (see page 72).

Reading: Matthew 16:13-17 (*NRSV*); Philippians 2:12-13

Now when Jesus came into the district of Caesarea Philippi, he asked his disciples, 'Who do people say that the Son of Man is?' And they said, 'Some say John the Baptist, but others Elijah, and still others Jeremiah or one of the prophets.' He said to them, 'But who do you say that I am?' Simon Peter answered, 'You are the Messiah, the Son of the living God.' And Jesus answered him, 'Blessed are you, Simon son of Jonah! For flesh and blood has not revealed this to you, but my Father in heaven.'

You must work out your own salvation with fear and trembling, recognising that God is at work in you so that you will be able to understand and accomplish his good purpose.

Comment

Are you a fan of Michael Palin's travel stories? Through series like *Full Circle, Around the World in 80 Days, Pole to Pole* and *Hemingway Adventure,* TV viewers have been treated to a taste of countries and cultures across the world, so that they can almost believe they have visited them personally. Almost, but not quite, for nothing, of course, can substitute for the real thing. Watching scenes of the North Pole from the warmth of our living room is far removed from struggling mile upon mile across frozen ice-sheets, exposed to subzero temperatures and the full force of Arctic gales. Seeing shots of the desert while cooled by an electric fan and sipping an iced drink is altogether different from gasping for water beneath a scorching relentless sun. The only way we can know what it is like to be somewhere is to be there ourselves. We may enter vicariously in a journey, but it will always be a second-hand experience unless we make it our own.

The same is true when it comes to Christian discipleship. Faith is not just *a* journey; it needs also to be *our* journey. That may sound like stating the obvious, for how can it be anything else? Yet the reality is that faith can all too easily become a borrowed experience. Proof of that can be seen in recent religious surveys. Most people in the UK still, it seems, consider themselves Christians, but how many are actually committed to Christ? If church attendance is anything to go by, the answer is precious few. Most people will freely admit that they only attend church for the so-called 'hatch, match and despatch' occasions – that is, christenings, weddings and funerals. Not that this is the ultimate yardstick, but it's a fair indication of where people stand. Faith for many is purely nominal, unrelated to daily life, based on some vague belief in God and the fact that we live in a supposedly Christian country. Others appeal to the fact that they were taught about faith as a child, brought up in a Christian home or attended Sunday school, faith seen as learned rather than experienced; some*thing* we know *about* rather than some*one* we know *personally*.

As we observed earlier, however, knowing about something is nothing like knowing it from experience. A good example of that is the trial of the Apostle Paul before the Roman governor Felix, recorded in Acts 24. Felix, we are told, 'was rather well informed about the Way' (Acts 24:22, *NRSV*), but that did not make him a Christian. Far from it – though he was happy enough to talk about faith on an abstract level, when Paul confronted him with the challenge of the gospel in terms of daily life – issues such as 'justice, self-control, and the coming judgement' (Acts 24:25, *NRSV*) – he didn't want to know, swiftly adjourning the trial and sending Paul back to prison. Although Paul was ostensibly the one on trial, Felix was the one facing important questions, and he didn't like it one bit. The scenario was to be repeated before Herod Agrippa, a Jew well schooled in Jewish tradition and well aware of the message concerning Jesus. As Paul challenges him concerning his faith, he responds defensively, 'Are you so quickly persuading me to become a Christian?' to which Paul replies, 'Whether quickly or not, I pray to God that not only you but also all who are listening to me today might become such as I am – except for these chains' (Acts 26:28-29, *NRSV*).

Both Herod and Agrippa knew *about* Jesus – the claims made for him and the claims he had made for himself – but this did not mean they could call themselves Christians. To do that, they would have needed to respond. So it was also for the disciples, in the incident recorded in the first part of our reading. Having followed Jesus for some time – watching, listening, learning – they were well aware of what people were saying about him – the rumour, gossip and speculation. Like few others, they had been privileged to share with him in a unique way, yet they still had to take a further step: to make up their minds concerning who Jesus was and what he meant for them. 'Who do people say that the Son of Man is?' asks Jesus, and they answer, 'Some say John the Baptist, but others Elijah, and still others Jeremiah or one of the prophets' (Matthew 16:13b-14, *NRSV*). Then comes the crunch question: 'But who do *you* say that I am?' (Matthew 16:15b, *NRSV*, italics added). Suddenly, it's no longer about others but about *them*, what *they* believe, and, as so often, Peter takes the lead, happy to declare his faith and personally respond. That's what faith is about, and that's what underlies a moment of conversion or public act of commitment: recognising that discipleship is not about *any* journey but *our* journey. Faith can never rest on someone else's experience, on what others have told us about Christ – it needs to be true for us!

If, though, our response is a personal matter, so also is our journey. It is surely this that Paul was talking about in those words to the Philippians: 'You must work out your own salvation with fear and trembling, recognising that God is at work in you so that you will be able to understand and accomplish his good purpose' (Philippians 2:12). We can interpret that challenge in various ways, but for me the important thing is the emphasis once more upon the personal, upon our *own* relationship with God, only this time in the sense of an ongoing commitment rather than single response. The disciples walked and talked with Jesus in Palestine, sharing personally in his ministry, witnessing his life and death. Paul, by contrast, was from Tarsus, never meeting or knowing Jesus in the flesh, yet, like the disciples, he experienced a powerful life-changing meeting with the risen Christ. Those to whom he preached were Jews and Gentiles, individuals from different countries and cultures, with sharply contrasting backgrounds and ideas, and correspondingly different experiences. Some would have interpreted their experience in one way, some in another; some had this gift, some had that – although they worshipped the same Lord and shared the one faith, each worked that out through a personal and individual journey. So it is for us, in turn. We are not meant to be exact replicas of each other, all believing precisely the same thing, worshipping in a uniform fashion, expressing ourselves in identical ways. Faith is a journey, and for each one that journey is different. There is no blueprint, no single path that everyone must take – just as we are all unique, so our experience of God is unique also!

A personal response leading to a personal journey – but one thing else must be said: that journey must affect us *personally*. Many of us, like Felix and Agrippa, are happy to talk about Jesus so long as it does not impinge upon our private life or ask too much of us. Such a response may be the most comfortable but it has little to do with faith. True discipleship means allowing our lives to be examined and transformed, opening ourselves to the searching gaze of Christ and listening to what he has to say, even when his message is unwelcome and disturbing. It means reflecting on the people we are, assessing how we think, talk and act, and striving to become more like Jesus. It means following the way of love, reaching out in faith, proclaiming the gospel in word and deed. True discipleship necessarily touches anything and everything, no part of life left untouched. If it doesn't do that, something is badly wrong.

'Who do you say I am?' Jesus asked his disciples, and he goes on asking the same of us today. Not, 'Who do *others* say?' Not, 'Who have you been *told* I am?' Not, 'Who am I *meant* to be?' But who do *you* say?' Have you answered that question? Is yours a personal journey of faith?

Summary

- There's no substitute for personal experience. Hearing or seeing about someone else's journey is not the same as journeying ourselves.
- The same is true of the journey of discipleship. Faith must be about *our* journey rather than that of others. Many consider

themselves Christians because they once went to Sunday school, know a little about the Bible or live in a 'Christian' country. They confuse nominal Christianity with committed discipleship.

- Felix and Agrippa, two of those who heard the charges brought against Paul in Rome, were both well acquainted with the Way of Christ. The fact that they knew *about* it did not, though, make them Christians. True faith is not about knowing some*thing* but some*one*. It involves an act of personal commitment, a response as individuals to Christ.

- In contrast to Felix and Agrippa, the Apostles, with Simon Peter acting as their spokesman, faced up to the personal challenge of Jesus.

- Faith also involves a personal journey going beyond that initial act of commitment. As Paul puts it, we must work out our own salvation. No two of us are the same; we will all experience God in different ways and interpret our experiences according to our own situation.

- Finally, faith must affect us *personally*. The journey must necessarily affect every part of life, shaping who and what we are. The gospel brings a challenge to our lifestyle and a change in direction from the old way to the new.

- 'Who do you say that I am?' That is the question of Jesus not just to the disciples but also to you and me today. Not who do others say, but who do *you* say that I am? Have we answered that question? Is faith for us about a personal journey?

Discussion

- Have you made a personal act of commitment, or does your faith rest on what others have told you? Have you discovered for yourself the reality of Jesus in your life?

- In what ways does Christian commitment make a difference in your life? How far does your faith show itself in action?

- Is your faith a theoretical exercise or a life-changing personal encounter? Are you willing to let it speak directly to your life rather than talk generally about all?

Prayer

Lord Jesus Christ,
    we talk of following you,
    but so often reality falls short of the ideal.
Instead of responding to your guidance we prefer our own way,
    pursuing our own goals,
    following our own inclinations.
We turn to you as and when it suits us,
    most often in times of need, when we have lost our way,
    only to abandon you again once you set us on our feet.
Yet we still expect you to be there when we need you,
    ready to answer our prayers and grant your blessing
    despite our slowness to serve you.
Forgive us for seeing faith as something given to us on a plate
    rather than something we need to work at;
    for acting as though all it requires
    is a one-off moment of conversion
    rather than a continuing story of commitment.
Teach us that it must be rooted in personal experience
    rather than the testimony of others.
Help us, then, to open our hearts to you,
    so that we may not simply know about you,
    but truly know you as our personal Saviour, Lord and friend,
    through your grace.
Amen.

Meditation of Peter

I thought he was just curious, at the start,
    interested in the latest gossip,
    the rumours circulating among the crowds –
    wouldn't you have wanted to know, in his shoes?
So we told him what folk were saying –
    'Some say John the Baptist,
    others Elijah,
    others Jeremiah, or one of the prophets.'
He smiled at that,
    clearly unsurprised,
    and it dawned on us that this hadn't been the real question,
    just leading up to the one that mattered.
'And what about you?' he said.
'Who do *you* say I am?'
A challenge that changed everything,
    for suddenly he wasn't simply asking about *others*
    but about *us* –
    where *we* stood,
    what *we* thought!
We'd been content until then to stay in the wings,
    observing rather than involved,
    watching from the sidelines rather than standing alongside,
    but the time had come to decide.
It was no longer sufficient to dip our feet in,
    test the waters;
    we had to take the plunge,
    sink or swim –
    and, put like that, I for one had no hesitation.
We knew already he was special, of course,
    that much clear from the beginning,
    an air about him,
    almost an aura, you might say,
    setting him apart,
    speaking of authority,

wisdom,
love –
in short, of God;
and I'd followed him because of it,
attracted,
intrigued,
eager to learn more.
But the Messiah? –
God's chosen one? –
could that really be?
I had my doubts, even then,
much that wasn't clear,
but I understood enough to grasp he offered
what no one else could:
a hope, love and life unlike anything I'd ever glimpsed before,
so I opened my heart,
declared my faith
and offered my commitment.
It's been difficult sometimes – I must be honest –
and I still lose my way,
still stray from the path,
but it's been wonderful, too,
the best decision I've ever made,
for I've not only followed him on *his* journey,
he's also become part of *mine*!

Further reading: John 1:10-13

He was in the world, and the world came into being through him;
yet the world did not know him. He came to what was his own,
and his own people did not accept him. But to all who received
him and believed in his name, he gave power to become children
of God, who were born not of blood or of the will of the flesh, or of
the will of man, but of God. (*NRSV*)

Suggestions for action

Reflect on how far your faith is your own, and how far it affects you personally. If it's not, or it doesn't, assess where changes need to be made, and personally recommit your life to Christ.

Closing prayer

Living God,
 teach us to base our faith not simply on the testimony of others,
 but on a personal experience of Christ,
 and so may we follow him
 and walk with you,
 this and every day.
Amen.

Third week

Equipped for the journey

Opening prayer

May the strength of God lead me,
   may the power of God preserve me,
   may the wisdom of God instruct me,
   may the hand of God protect me,
   may the way of God direct me,
   may the shield of God defend me,
   may the hosts of God guard me
   against the snares of evil
   and the temptations of the world.
In your salvation, O Lord, always be mine,
   this day and for evermore.
Amen.

St Patrick

Introduction

'This is strange,' I thought. 'Why is the car so difficult to drive today?' And then it dawned on me. I'd been to the local quarry to buy some stones for a rock garden I was constructing, and was returning with the boot well loaded. I hadn't intended to buy more than a few bagfuls, but the quarry had stipulated a minimum purchase of so many hundredweight, and so, unthinkingly, I'd kept on piling rocks in until I reached this target. It had seemed a bargain at the time, but driving home I wasn't so sure, for I was struggling to keep the car on the road. Almost certainly, the weight was beyond the safe limit. Worse still, it was all at the back of the vehicle, making steering virtually impossible. The few miles home took what seemed like an eternity as I crept along at a snail's pace, ignoring the glares and gestures of frustrated drivers as they waited impatiently for an opportunity to overtake me. That day brought home to me the potentially catastrophic consequences of being overloaded on a journey, and I resolved never to make the same mistake again.

In some ways, though, we can do something very similar in the journey of life, as became all too clear to me when I last moved house. For weeks beforehand, my wife and I were busy sorting through clutter – box after box of books, papers, ornaments and general bits and pieces. It was astonishing to discover how quickly it had all built up, but even more astonishing to find how little we actually needed. There were files of notes dating back to my college days that I'd scarcely looked at since and would certainly never look at again. There were books by the barrow load that I'd never even opened let alone read, most of them only there for show, to create a good impression should a senior colleague happen to pop in! Most of all, there was simply bric-a-brac: broken tools and gadgets stuffed away in a drawer in case they might one day prove useful, out-of-date seeds that hadn't the remotest chance of germinating, letters I'd meant to reply to, pile upon pile of photographs, unwanted ornaments and pictures given as Christmas presents – all kinds of rubbish cluttering up the garage, loft, cupboards and study, gathering dust and generally getting in the way.

Why do we fill our homes with such things? Why do we buy them in the first place? Sometimes, of course, they are given to us as presents and kept because of special associations and sentimental value, but many of our possessions are bought on the spur of the moment, not because we need them but because we want them or simply because they briefly tickle our fancy. Whatever our reasons, we are reluctant to let some things go once we have bought them, most of us deriving a sense of security from being surrounded by possessions. Yet are these important? Do they offer security and happiness? More often than not the opposite is true, possessions a millstone round our neck instead of a source of pleasure. A good clear-out brings a wonderful sense of liberation; until, that is, we settle down and accumulate it all once again!

So what do we need in the journey of faith? What things are essentials and which are trivia? It is a question we need to answer.

Activity

Choices (see page 73).

Reading: Matthew 10:8b-10; Ephesians 6:11-18a

You have received freely; give freely in turn. Take no gold, silver or copper coins in your belts, no wallet for your journey, no spare tunic, sandals or a staff, for workers deserve their food . . . Don the whole armour of God, so that you may be able to withstand the ruses of the devil. For we do battle, not with flesh and blood, but with the rulers, authorities and cosmic powers of darkness – with the spiritual forces of evil in high places. Take up, then, the whole armour of God, so that you may be able to resist on that evil day, and, having done everything, still stand resolute. Stand, therefore, and secure the belt of truth around your waist, and put on the breastplate of righteousness. Shoe your feet with a readiness to proclaim the gospel of peace. Above all, grasp the shield of faith, with which you will be able to smother the flaming arrows of the evil one. Take also, by prayer and supplication, the helmet of salvation, and the sword of the Spirit, which is the word of God.

Comment

Every year I look forward to going on holiday, and every year there's just one fly in the ointment – packing. It's hard enough deciding what and what not to take, especially if, like my wife and me, you choose to stay somewhere in this country. Such are the vagaries of the British climate that even in high summer you have to be prepared for both sunshine and rain, heat wave and cold snap, so into the suitcase goes a mixture of tee shirts and woolly jumpers, beach shoes and wellington boots, sun cream and water-proofs. Loath to be caught short, we do our best to prepare for every eventuality; only then, of course, comes the nightmare of trying to squeeze everything into the car, and the realisation that some things simply won't fit. As a boy, it was even worse. My parents didn't drive, so for every holiday we had to rely on public transport. There could be no stuffing of bags, cases, footballs and food supplies into the boot; each of us had our share of items to carry, staggering under the weight of bulging suitcases from house to station and from station to holiday flat.

The answer, of course, is to take as little as possible, but what happens then? You've guessed it: the items you decide to leave behind are precisely those you later discover you need! Fine though it sounds in theory to travel light, some things are simply indispen-sable for a journey. Imagine, for example, walking in the mountains without a map or sturdy pair of walking shoes; you'd soon meet with disaster. Imagine caving or potholing without a torch and helmet; it would be asking for trouble. Imagine going abroad without money, credit card or travellers' cheques, and a passport and visa; you either wouldn't reach your destination or would be financially embarrassed when you did. Whatever the journey might be, we need to be equipped for it, prepared for the circumstances we are likely to meet, and to venture out unprepared is foolhardy indeed.

We are faced, then, with a conundrum. We need enough, but not too much – what is essential rather than superfluous? So it is also in Christian discipleship as we walk the way of Christ. Too often we can be weighed down by heavy burdens, refusing to let go of what is finally unnecessary, but we can equally find our-selves caught short, unprepared to face the challenges life brings. The dichotomy is well captured in the two passages that comprise our reading above. On the one hand, we have Jesus sending out his disciples with the words, 'You have received freely; give freely in turn. Take no gold, silver or copper coins in your belts, no wallet for your journey, no spare tunic, sandals or a staff, for workers deserve their food' (Matthew 10:8-10). On the other hand, we have Paul exhorting Christians to 'take up the whole armour of God', wearing 'the belt of truth', 'the breastplate of righteousness' and 'the helmet of salvation', our feet shod in readiness while grasping 'the shield of faith' and 'the sword of the Spirit'. There is, though, no contradiction here. Both are making the same point but approaching it from different perspectives, Jesus concerned with physical possessions and Paul with spiritual resources.

With Jesus, the emphasis is on travelling light, letting go of everything that may hold us down and prevent us from fulfilling our appointed task. What does that mean for us in practice? Should we sell everything we have, as Jesus counselled the rich young ruler, throwing ourselves in faith upon the charity of others? That may be the way for some, but it can't be for all, or else there would be no charity to give, nothing to provide for the needs of anyone. The problem facing the rich ruler was not his riches as such, but the fact that they held him captive, taking priority in his life. Though he ostensibly possessed them, the truth was that *they* possessed *him*, and until they stopped being his ultimate goal, taking precedence over everything else, he would always struggle to follow Jesus, for there would be too much to distract him from his path. Certainly giving to others is part of discipleship, and a major part at that, but the thrust of what Jesus is saying is that physical possessions of any kind cannot meet our needs, the resources required for the journey of faith coming from God, not ourselves. The lesson is reminiscent of the prophet Isaiah: 'Why spend your money on that which is not bread, and why offer your labour for that which cannot satisfy? Listen carefully to what I say, and you will eat what is good, delighting yourselves in the richest of food' (Isaiah 55:2). Not only is it true that material possessions can never finally buy happiness, they can also actually destroy it, so concerned do we become with acquiring, safeguarding and preserving them. To be effective in discipleship, to grow in our faith and to discover lasting happiness, we need to break free of the stranglehold of possessions, recognising that our ultimate security lies elsewhere. We need to be ready to use them not for our own ends but in the service of Christ. That may sound easy enough, but how much would we be willing to renounce should we be put to the test?

The emphasis of Paul is slightly different, focusing on what we need to put on rather than take off. 'Take up the whole armour of God,' he tells us, 'so that you may be able to resist on that evil day, and, having done everything, still stand resolute' (Ephesians 6:13). Paul knew only too well the challenges and pressures and demands of Christian life, and so he lists here the resources God has placed at our disposal. We can analyse and draw lessons from each one – truth, righteousness, the gospel of peace, faith, salvation, the Holy Spirit, the word of God and prayer – but the important thing is that these are God-given resources, unlike anything the world can give. Resources like these do not weigh us down or hold us back, but give us the strength we need for the journey, offering protection, sustenance and guidance to see us through. They are part of the easy yoke and light burden that Jesus spoke of, for in reality we do not carry *them; they* carry us. Yet if God provides them for our use, it is up to us to put them on, and to do that we do not simply slip them on or pick them up off the shelf; it is a continuing process, something we go on doing each day, so that faith is constantly renewed. Unless we make time for prayer and God's word, unless we open our lives to the breath of the Spirit, unless we seek truth and hunger and thirst after righteousness, unless we respond personally to the gospel working out our salvation, we will founder and stumble on our journey.

What, then, of you? Where do your priorities lie: in the things of this world or the things of God, in earthly riches or spiritual treasure; in material security or the armour that God alone provides? What are you taking for your journey, and will it hold you back or spur you forward? Are you equipped to follow the way of Christ?

Summary

- It is tempting sometimes to take too much for a journey, ensuring we are covered against every eventuality. Equally, we can take too little, so that we come up against circumstances for which we are unprepared.

- Both points apply to the journey of discipleship. On the one hand, Jesus tells us to travel light, warning against the danger of possessions. On the other hand, we need to put on the armour of God, if we are to be properly prepared to walk the way of Christ. These are two aspects of the same truth.

- On one level, the words of Jesus to his disciples were purely practical, warning them against loading themselves down with unnecessary baggage and so impeding their journey. On another level, though, he is emphasising that we need to trust in God's provision rather than our own. His words to the rich ruler who came seeking eternal life bring out this truth further. Riches and possessions may be attractive but they cannot finally satisfy. Worse than that, they may close our minds to what is important, to the things of God. Outwardly we may have plenty but inwardly be empty, searching for meaning and spiritual fulfilment. We need to let go and trust in the resources God provides.

- These are precisely the resources that Paul focuses on in his words to the Ephesians. We have the armour of God at our disposal to equip us for the journey. Though this is God-given, we have to put it on ourselves, and continue putting it on each day. It is through focusing on the things of God and making them our own that we will find what we need to walk the way of Christ.

Discussion

- How much do possessions really mean to us? How far do our lives reflect this? What things would we find hardest to let go of? What does it mean to live by faith?

- In what ways do possessions obscure more important things in life? Is this merely fine-sounding rhetoric? Have any of us ever consciously given something up or denied ourselves out of principle?
- What do we see as the armour of God? Do we make sufficient time and space in our lives to put this on? What pieces of armour do we consider most important?

Prayer

Living God,
  we tell ourselves that possessions aren't important to us,
  but the reality is all too often different.
We cling to the security afforded by our belongings,
  pinning our security on worldly wealth
  and constantly striving after more,
  closing our eyes to what is ultimately important in life.
Forgive us the time, money and resources we waste
  in accumulating what we do not need.
Forgive the selfishness that lies behind this,
  and the wasted opportunities to give from our plenty.
Teach us to travel light,
  recognising where true fulfilment lies
  and where true strength can be found,
  and so may our service be deepened
  and our relationship with you enriched,
  through the grace of Jesus Christ.
Amen.

Meditation of Matthew

'Take no coins in your belts,
  no wallet for your journey,
  no spare tunic, sandals or a staff.'

Could he be serious, I wondered?
Surely not!
But he *was* –
    we were to travel in faith,
    confident that somewhere, somehow,
    our needs would be met.
Well, my heart sank, you can imagine –
    to set off on a journey
    not knowing were the next meal is coming from,
    without a shekel to your name,
    not to mention a change of clothing –
    that takes some doing, believe me!
He was right, though – I came to see that later –
    for it taught us not simply to live by faith,
    important though that can be,
    but to sort out our priorities
    and to travel light.
You see, we couldn't have gone far with a load on our backs,
    a sackful of provisions.
We had to be free,
    unencumbered,
    able to stride out wherever he might lead us –
    and that's what we did,
    not just then, but later,
    going out in his name to proclaim his word.
Yet that's not the end of it,
    for those words of his were not simply for us but for you,
    as much about *your* journey as any.
'Do not worry about what you will eat, drink, wear,' he had said,
    'but seek first the kingdom of God and his righteousness
    and you will receive all these as well.'
'Sell everything, and give to the poor;
    then come, follow me.'
'Come to me all you who are tired of carrying heavy loads
    and I will give you rest –
    take my yoke on you and learn from me,

for my yoke is easy
and my burden is light.'
In other words, let go of everything that binds us to earth,
 that weighs us down and holds us back:
  the grasping for riches and clinging to possessions
  that consumes not just so much of our time but our very selves,
  leaving us empty instead of full,
  hungry instead of satisfied.
Focus instead on the things that matter,
 the resources he provides,
 the true essentials of life.
I'm not telling you what to take for *your* journey –
 that's between you and him –
 but don't confuse what you want with what you need,
 what will see you through with what will hold you back,
 or else, far from being ready to travel,
 you may find yourself ready to drop,
 and with nothing and no one to pick you up.

Further reading: Matthew 11:28-30, *NRSV*; Romans 13:12

Come to me, all you that are weary and are carrying heavy burdens, and I will give you rest. Take my yoke upon you, and learn from me; for I am gentle and humble in heart, and you will find rest for your souls. For my yoke is easy, and my burden is light . . . The night is nearly over, daybreak is near, so let us . . . put on the armour of light.

Suggestions for action

Make time for prayer, Bible study, personal devotion and public worship. Stop striving after possessions, let go of the things you don't need, and focus instead on what really matters in life.

Closing prayer

Living God,
    equip us, by the grace of Christ,
    and through the power of your Spirit,
    so that we may return confidently to our journey,
    and walk it faithfully each day,
    to the glory of your name.
Amen.

Fourth week

A journey of discovery

Opening prayer

Lord God,
  the protector of all who trust in you,
  without whom nothing is strong,
  nothing is holy,
  increase and multiply upon us your mercy
  that you, being our ruler and guide,
  we may pass through things temporal
  that we finally lose not the things eternal.
Grant this, heavenly Father,
  for the sake of Jesus Christ our Lord.
Amen.

Daily Office Revised

Introduction

I was in a computer shop the other day, waiting to be served. It proved to be a long wait, for the customer in front of me had a long list of questions to which she sought answers, understandably so, given that she was spending several hundred pounds on a new computer system. She didn't just want any old machine, but one that was up to spec, including features such as a modem for internet use, the latest editions of Microsoft Windows and Word, a zip drive and a CD rewriter, to name but a few. Nothing remarkable in that, you might think, except that I've omitted one detail – the woman in question was in her late eighties! It was heart-warming to hear the interest and enthusiasm in her voice, and to know that here was someone whose mind was still young, even if her body was advancing in years. If I survive into old age, with all my faculties intact, I hope that I will possess the same openness to accept new ideas, the same eagerness to learn more, and the same willingness to have my horizons stretched and challenged.

We need similar qualities when it comes to the journey of discipleship, for instead of growing mature as Christians we can so easily simply grow old, no longer open to the renewing power of Christ or the life-giving breath of his Spirit. Faith can never stand still but should constantly be growing, deepened each day by new experiences of God's love. Neither should it reach a point where we consider it complete or immutable, for that is to limit God to our own understanding. Whatever we have learned, there is still more to discover. However far we have come, there is still further to go. In the words of George Rawson's old hymn, 'The Lord has yet more light and truth to break forth from his word.'

Activity

Explorers quiz (see page 74).

Reading: Philippians 3:10-14

I want to know Christ and the power of his resurrection and what it means to participate in his sufferings through identifying with him in his death; if, through that, I may somehow attain to the resurrection from the dead. Not that I have already achieved this or reached such a goal, but I endeavour continually to make it my own, just as Christ Jesus has made me his own. Friends, I do not claim to have yet secured this for myself; but what I do is this: forgetting what is past and straining forward to what is yet in store, I strive to reach the goal of the prize of God's heavenly call in Christ Jesus.

Comment

Do you have the makings of an explorer? I wish I had, and, yes, perhaps part of me hankers after excitement and adventure – the thrill of hacking through the jungle, struggling across polar icecaps or trudging through unexplored deserts – but only a small part of me! Most of the time I'm quite happy to be boring but safe! If what I'm told of my ancestry is correct, however, I should perhaps be a little more adventurous, for one of my distant relations is reputedly Colonel Percy Fawcett, an intrepid explorer hailing from Torquay in Devon, who, together with his eldest son, set off in 1925 to explore the jungles of Mato Grosso, where he disappeared without trace. I must confess that I have never investigated whether or not I am truly related to Percy, nor have I read the book *Exploration Fawcett*, despite it having sat on a shelf for many years, but a couple of photos in that book bear an uncanny resemblance to my father, so if you hear one day that I've set off for Timbuktu, don't be entirely surprised!

In one sense, though, we are all called to be explorers, and that, of course, is in the unfolding journey of faith. We have already looked at the example of Abraham in an earlier session, noting his willingness to set off into the unknown. So it was to be for the disciples, each called to leave their old way of life and follow Jesus. In this session, though, I want to focus on two people in particular – Simon Peter and Paul – for theirs, like few others, are stories of faith as an evolving pilgrimage.

Had you asked Peter who he believed Jesus was when he was first asked to follow, how would he have answered? He was in awe, certainly, recognising that Jesus spoke with the authority of God, but did he recognise him as the Messiah? Not yet – that was to come later. At first he was simply a charismatic figure whose sheer presence inspired him to follow – special, undoubtedly, worth following, but exactly who he was he couldn't have said. Then, as the days passed and he witnessed Jesus' ministry first-hand, so what he believed took shape. First, perhaps, Jesus was a teacher, his words possessing such authority they couldn't be ignored;

then a worker of miracles, able to do amazing signs and wonders; then one who would deliver his country from Roman oppression; and then came that decisive moment when he acknowledged Jesus as the Christ, God's promised Messiah. Yet that was not the end of the journey – just another step along the road. The idea that he understood who Jesus was more clearly than the other disciples did is given the lie in what follows, when far from being the rock of the Church, as Jesus first describes him, he is labelled 'Satan'. Strong stuff indeed! If he thought he had understood the nature of Christ, he was given a rude awakening. It was a similar story later, Peter emphatically declaring undying allegiance, only to deny his faith shortly afterwards. In the space of a few weeks, he was to see Jesus as the one done to death on a cross, then the risen Christ, and, finally, the sovereign ascended Lord! Yet, even then, there was more to learn, more to experience and more to understand, as seen particularly in his encounter with Cornelius; an encounter that brought home to him that the gospel was for Gentile as well as Jew, not just for some but all. There was no point at which he could claim to have understood everything there was to understand; no point when he had exhausted all that faith had to offer. Faith was never a finished article but always on the production line, being shaped, added to, refined, polished.

The same was to be true for the Apostle Paul, a similar sense of anticipation characterising his writing. 'For the moment,' he wrote to the Corinthians, 'we see but a riddle in a mirror, then we shall see face to face; now I see only in part, but then I will fully know just as I am fully known' (1 Corinthians 13:12). For all his wisdom, knowledge and understanding, Paul recognised that there was much still beyond him, far more than he could ever begin to comprehend. 'O, the depth of the riches of the wisdom and knowledge of God!' he wrote in his letter to the Romans (11:33-34). 'How unfathomable are his judgements, and mysterious are his ways! Who has known the mind of the Lord, or who can claim to have been his counsellor?' Yet if complete knowledge would always be out of reach, this did not mean he would stop searching for it, striving each day to deepen his understanding and to experience more of the reality of

Christ within his life. So those wonderful words to the Philippians (3:10-14), 'I want to know Christ and the power of his resurrection and what it means to participate in his sufferings through identifying with him in his death; if, through that, I may somehow attain to the resurrection from the dead. Not that I have already achieved this or reached such a goal, but I endeavour continually to make it my own, just as Christ Jesus has made me his own. Friends, I do not claim to have yet secured this for myself; but what I do is this: forgetting what is past and straining forward to what is yet in store, I strive to reach the goal of the prize of God's heavenly call in Christ Jesus.' For Paul, faith was a constant adventure; being a Christian was a life of never-ending discovery. In his judgement, no words could do justice to everything God had done in Christ. The more he understood, the more he realised he had yet to learn. His words to the Ephesians (3:17-19) applied as much to him as them: 'I pray . . . that Christ may so dwell in your hearts through faith that you will be able to grasp with all the saints the breadth, length, height and depth of the love of Christ; and that you may know this all-surpassing love in such a way that you will be filled with the very fullness of God.'

If that was so for Paul – a man who perhaps did more than any other to spread the gospel and advance the Christian faith – then how much more so should it be for us? However much we may know of Christ, however mature and advanced in faith, there is still much more to learn. We may have been a Christian six months, six years or sixty years; there is still more to discover. We may be the keenest of scholars or most distinguished of theologians; we will still have only skimmed the surface. All of us are called to be explorers, embarked on an adventure of faith, a lifetime's pilgrimage. Faith can never be static, something that we can neatly place in a box saying, 'There it is'. It is something constantly growing, changing, maturing and evolving, always ready to be taken one step further as new dimensions unfold and new aspects of truth are revealed.

What, then, of us? Are we ready, if necessary, to step out in faith? Are we prepared, should God ask it, to let go of the familiar

47

and explore the unknown? Are we willing to consider new ideas, challenges and initiatives, not knowing where they will lead or what they will demand from us? When God calls, are we ready to respond and follow in faith? However long we have travelled the way of Christ and however rich our experience may have been, the journey is not yet over. There are new discoveries to be made and new horizons to explore. Are we ready to meet them?

Summary

- We may not all be intrepid explorers but we are all called to explore our faith.
- The experience of Simon Peter exemplifies how faith grows and develops across the years. He began by following Jesus without really understanding who he was. Even when he confessed faith in Jesus as the Messiah, his understanding was still flawed, finding it impossible to accept that Jesus must suffer and die. In the week leading up to the cross, Peter believed he had learned his lesson, but events were to prove him wrong, his denial of Jesus exposing the weakness of his commitment. Even following the resurrection and Ascension, Peter was still learning, as can be seen in the story of Cornelius. Faith never stood still; it was always being taken a step further.
- So too with the Apostle Paul. Deep though his faith was, he knew that in this life it would always be imperfect. He had more to learn, further to progress, and he strove constantly to a deeper knowledge of Christ.
- The same should hold for us. However long we have been Christians, we can never claim to have arrived. We need always to be open to new ideas and horizons, prepared to face what might challenge and stretch our faith.

Discussion

* Have you lost sight of the need to grow in faith? Have you come to regard being a Christian as settling at a destination rather than progressing on a journey?
* In what ways might faith for us be a journey into the unknown?
* Are you genuinely open to where God might lead, or have you already decided where your journey of faith will take you?

Prayer

Lord,
>   you do not call us to a destination but a journey –
>   a continuing exploration of the wonder of your love.
Save us from ever thinking we have arrived,
>   from imagining we know all there is to know
>   or that we have exhausted the riches
>   of everything you would reveal to us.
Teach us that, however much we may understand,
>   there is always more to see,
>   more to learn
>   and more to understand.
Open our eyes to the great adventure of faith
>   and to the unfathomable mysteries of your purpose,
>   and so help us to live as pilgrim people,
>   travelling on to new horizons,
>   until we see and know you face to face
>   in the light of your kingdom,
>   and you are all in all.
Amen.

Meditation of Paul

I thought I knew him better than most,
    that over the years I'd come to understand him
    as few have even begun to.
And I suppose I had – to a point –
    for I'd glimpsed the wonder of his presence,
    I'd heard the sound of his voice,
    and, by his grace,
    I'd declared his purpose and made known his love:
    good news for all the world.
Impressed?
You shouldn't be –
    for it was nothing,
    just the merest glimmer of light,
    a tiny window on to an indescribable world of mystery.
Don't get me wrong, it was special in its way,
    every moment of my ministry a privilege
    which I shall always treasure,
    shaping my life and that of countless others.
I spoke of love, and my heart thrilled within me,
    leaping like a deer sensing streams of life-giving water.
I spoke of forgiveness,
    a fresh start,
    new beginnings for us all,
    and my spirit sang for joy,
    dancing in exultation.
I spoke of light shining in the darkness,
    reaching out into the gloom,
    reviving, renewing, restoring,
    and my mouth gave praise to God,
    a song on my lips and his word on my tongue.
Yes, it was magical, no question,
    enough to set my soul on fire and my heart ablaze,
    yet it was a fraction of the whole,
    a speck of flotsam in the vast and unfathomable ocean that is God.

Whatever I'd glimpsed, far more lay hidden;
   whatever I'd grasped, far more had yet to be revealed,
   whatever I thought I'd understood,
   there was more always out of reach,
   too awesome even to contemplate,
   for we were different, he God and I man,
   he before all and over all, sovereign over space and time,
   and me? –
   a fleeting breath,
   a passing shadow,
   like the flower of the field, here today and gone tomorrow.
I thought I knew him,
   and to be fair, I did, my knowledge of him growing each day –
   new insights,
   new discoveries,
   new wonders beyond imagining,
   but I recognise now that however far I've come
   there's further still to go,
   more yet to learn –
   for all my travelling, the journey's only just begun!

Further reading: 1 Corinthians 8:2

Those who imagine they have fully understood something, have not yet begun to understand it at all, but if anyone loves God, then that person is fully known by him.

Suggestions for action

Examine understandings of faith different to your own. Share in worship with Christians of other traditions, talk with those holding contrasting viewpoints, read books that stretch and challenge your faith.

Closing prayer

Sovereign God,
    open our hearts to all you have yet to say,
    yet to do
    and yet to teach.
Help us to recognise that, far from being over,
    our journey has barely started,
    and so may we continue to explore the wonder of your love
    and mystery of your gracious purpose,
    this day and for evermore.
Amen.

Fifth week

—————— Completing the journey ——————

Opening prayer

O Lord,
give us grace to walk before you
all the days of this our pilgrimage
with a good conscience and pure mind,
that when you appear to reward us according to our deeds,
we may rejoice and not be ashamed before you at your coming.
Grant this for the sake of Jesus Christ our Lord and Saviour.
Amen.

Christian Prayers (1566; language updated)

Introduction

One of my favourite authors is the travel writer Bill Bryson. I've just finished reading his book *A Walk in the Woods*, a hilarious account of his attempt, together with a friend, to walk the Appalachian Trail in America. The title conjures up a casual stroll, doesn't it, but don't be fooled. At around 2400 kilometres in length, the Appalachian Trail is the longest continuous footpath in the world. Add in the fact that the route largely comprises rugged mountains covered by dense bear-infested forests, and you get some idea of the challenge it presents. Nonetheless, when Bryson and his colleague set off, they were confident of successfully completing the trail from start to finish.

Such blithe self-assurance was soon to change. Staggering under the weight of hefty backpacks, plagued by unseasonable weather (including six-foot snowdrifts), and far more out of condition than either had realised, their progress proved frustratingly slow. When, after a solid month of trekking, they chanced upon a map showing the full length of the trail and realised that they had barely completed a fraction of the route, they abandoned their plan to walk its entire length and settled instead for selected sections. An apparently straightforward journey turned out to be a gruelling marathon.

The same can be true of the journey of faith. We may, at times, progress serenely on our way, but at other times the going is less smooth. We will face obstacles in our path, challenges to faith, pressures and demands that tax us to the limit. More dangerous still, we will need to wrestle with the twin monsters of familiarity and complacency: the tendency explored in the last session to assume we have seen all there is to see, and the beguiling voice within telling us that everything is all right even when we know that it is far from it. Over the course of this book so far, we have looked at the need to follow, to personally respond, to equip ourselves for the journey, and to be open to new horizons. This session reminds us that we ignore those needs at our peril.

Activity

Pop quiz (see page 75).

Reading: Colossians 2:6-7; 2 Timothy 4:9-11a

So then, having received Christ as Lord, continue to walk in him, rooted, growing and established in the faith he taught you, and overflowing with thanksgiving . . . Come to me as soon as you can, for Demas, in love with this present world, has forsaken me and gone to Thessalonica, while Crescens has left for Galatia and Titus for Dalmatia. Only Luke remains with me.

Comment

'I've started, so I'll finish' – words made famous by Magnus Magnusson in the TV quiz show *Mastermind*. He referred, of course, to finishing his question, but those words can be applied equally both to life in general and to Christian discipleship. It's easy to start something, a different matter to finish it. If you doubt that, watch a group of runners lining up for a marathon. All will have their dreams of glory, their secret hopes of surging in first place across the finishing line, but of those who begin the race many will probably not finish, some crashing out in exhaustion and others simply deciding it's not worth the effort. It takes dedication and commitment to stick to something and complete the course, whether that be a race or anything else, many beginning a venture full of enthusiasm only for their ardour to peter out halfway through.

Sadly that can be just as true in terms of faith. We eagerly commit ourselves to Christ, impulsively responding to the message of the gospel, only to realise after a time that we have taken on more than we first anticipated. Somehow, the energy that fired our faith in the early days of commitment seems to fizzle out, until eventually, instead of travelling forward, we stand still or even slip backwards, our progress halted by familiarity, complacency or world-weariness. The initial act of commitment is easy; it's in seeing it through that the real test comes.

The story of Demas clearly illustrates the point. He is not one of the big names of the New Testament; quite the contrary, he is mentioned just three times, but in those passing references a sobering tale emerges. We meet him first in Colossians 4:14, where Paul writes, 'Luke, the beloved physician, and Demas greet you.' It's not much to go on and yet it says more than we might imagine, for Demas here is listed among those who Paul counted as fellow-workers in the cause of the gospel, on a par with Mark cousin of Barnabas, Epaphras the man of prayer, Tychicus 'a beloved brother', and, of course, Luke the physician. So it is also with the second reference: 'Epaphras, my fellow-prisoner in Christ Jesus, sends greetings to you, and so do Mark, Aristarchus, Demas, and Luke, my fellow workers' (Philemon v. 23-24, *NRSV*). Demas, in other words, is in good company, playing an important part in the life of the early Church and highly regarded by Paul himself. He is one in whom Paul would have placed great hopes as a leader of the future, confident that his faith and commitment would serve as an example to others.

If that was the case, though, such early promise was not to be fulfilled, for the last mention of Demas paints a very different picture. 'Come to me as soon as you can, for Demas, in love with this present world, has forsaken me and gone to Thessalonica' (2 Timothy 4:9-10a). There is almost a plaintive air about this appeal to Timothy, a rare note of despondency and dejection, and I've no doubt that was due not so much to any loneliness that Paul was feeling as to his sorrow over what had become of Demas. In stark contrast to the innumerable examples of faith and perseverance in Paul's letters, all the causes for joy and thanksgiving, here is the other side of the coin: a man who fell away, who didn't finish the course, who lost his way on the path of Christian discipleship. Exactly why, we are not told; simply that he was 'in love with this present world'. Did he perhaps find the cost of discipleship too great, resenting the demands, responsibilities and sacrifices asked of him? Were the risks in being a Christian simply too many, Demas, having seen Paul and others imprisoned, beaten and even threatened with death, understandably concerned about his own safety? Did he find hostile responses hard to live with, more concerned with being accepted by others than accepted by Jesus? Or were there more subtle reasons behind his decline? Did he perhaps get his priorities wrong, so busy with Christian service that he failed to make time to feed himself spiritually? Was it that he slowly compromised the way of Christ with the way of the world, turning a blind eye to a weakness here, a fault there, the occasional giving way to temptation and isolated lapse into old ways, only for these to become the norm rather than the exception? Did he succumb to the desire for riches and possessions, for making his way in the world never mind what it cost? Or was it simply that he lost his faith, his initial enthusiasm soon wearing thin and his commitment exposed as superficial?

We will never know for sure, but what we do know is that Demas wasn't the only one to fall by the wayside. In his first letter to Timothy, Paul had written of other casualties, implicitly warning how easily it can happen to any of us. 'I am giving you these instructions, Timothy, in accordance with the prophecies made earlier about you, so that by following them you may fight the good fight, having faith and a good conscience. By rejecting conscience, certain persons have suffered shipwreck in the faith, among them are Hymenaeus and Alexander' (1 Timothy 1:18-20a, *NRSV*). Nor were these the first to fall away, a note in John's Gospel telling us, 'a number of disciples turned back and no longer followed him' (John 6:66). It is easy to make a commitment, much harder to honour it.

Sadly, that is as true today as it has ever been. If all those who've professed faith at evangelistic rallies or attended Sunday school over the years had continued in faith, our churches would be bulging at the seams. If all those who've been baptised or confirmed were still committed, Christianity would be a growing force in this country. The reality, of course, for most denominations, is a story of continuing decline. Many start out but many also fall away. Don't let that be true of us. It can happen more easily than we might imagine.

I've started, so I'll finish. Can we say that? We may have professed our faith in Christ and started out on the journey of discipleship but that is not what finally counts. What matters is whether we complete the course, whether having put our hands to something we are ready to follow it through. Is our faith able to stand the test of time? Will we be a casualty along the way, or one of those able to say with the Apostle Paul, 'I have fought the good fight, I have finished the race, I have kept the faith. From now on there is reserved for me the crown of righteousness, which the Lord, the righteous judge, will give to me on that day, and not only to me but also to all who have longed for his appearing' (2 Timothy 4:7-8, *NRSV*).

Summary

- It's easy to start something, much harder to finish it.

- That is as true of discipleship as anything. The enthusiasm that characterises the early days of faith can rapidly dissipate as faith comes up against the harsh realities of life.

- The story of Demas is a case in point. Mentioned just three times in the New Testament, on the first two occasions he is clearly a valued colleague of the Apostle Paul, playing a leading role in the life of the early Church. He is last mentioned, however, as someone who has fallen away, 'in love with the present world'. Somewhere along the path of discipleship, things had clearly gone wrong.

- We do not know where the problem lay, but his example shows that even those who seem most committed can lose their faith.

- Demas wasn't alone; many others also fell away. The same continues to be true today, many coming to faith but not all continuing in it.

- The same can happen to us more easily than we might imagine. Familiarity and complacency in particular can undermine our commitment.

- Will we be able to finish what we've started? Are we, like the Apostle Paul, committed to running the race to the very end?

Discussion

- What do you think causes people today to fall away from faith? Why is it that many never come to faith at all?

- Have there been times when you personally had to work through difficult patches when your faith seemed threatened? What was the cause of this? What obstacles did you come up against? What helped you to come through?

- What do you think is most important in keeping faith fresh and alive? Which of the four themes covered so far in this book is most important in contributing towards that?

Prayer

Living God,
  we have committed ourselves to the path of discipleship
  and we want to walk it faithfully,
  but we know how easy it is to slip back.
When your message is too demanding,
  when you ask from us what we would rather not give,
  and when your words make us feel uncomfortable,
  striking too near the mark,
  then we turn away from you, resisting your call.
When other interests conflict with discipleship,
  when the demands and responsibilities of each day
  crowd in upon us,
  we are swift to forget you,
  ignoring your will in preference to our own.
When life is hard and things do not go as we hope,
  faith gives way to doubt and we lose sight of your promises.
Forgive us the shallowness of our commitment,
  and help us constantly to be alert to that danger,
  able to recognise those things that might trip us up
  and cause us to fall.
Hold on to us,
  keep us steady,
  and direct our footsteps,
  and if we stumble, lead us on to the way of life once more
  and grant that we may continue safely on our way
  until our journey's end.
In the name of Christ we ask it.
Amen.

Meditation of Demas

Don't be too hard on me.
I know I've failed, all too well.
No need for you to twist the knife –
    I do that myself every day.
Demas, the man who fell away –
    that's what they'll call me:
    the man who couldn't stay the course,
    who found the going too tough.
I can see it all now –
    they'll preach sermons about me,
    warning against falling away,
    turning back,
    and though none of them knows just why it happened
    they'll make their guesses:
    cowardice,
    doubt,
    weakness,
    ambition –
    plenty to choose from.
They're right . . . and wrong,
    for it wasn't just one of those
    but all of them put together,
    slowly but surely eroding faith.
I was afraid of the cost,
    terrified at the thought of pain,
    the prospect of death.
I had my doubts,
    all too many,
    a host of questions unresolved.
Weak?
Of course I was –
    careless in devotion,
    feeble in self-discipline,
    too easily led astray.

And ambitious?
Certainly.
I was eager to get on in the world,
    anxious to keep in with the right people,
    and concerned that commitment to Christ
    might give the wrong idea.
Yet if that was true of me, it was true also of others,
    but they still follow,
    still trust,
    so why not me?
I wish I knew,
    I really do,
    but I just can't say.
Somehow the magic's gone,
    the sparkle that made faith come alive,
    and though I could pretend it's there,
    put on a front and claim I still believe,
    what would be the point?
I might deceive others,
    perhaps in time even fool myself,
    but not Jesus,
    not him.
I know I've failed,
    he knows I've failed,
    and I can only pray that he will accept me now
    as he accepted me then,
    despite myself.

Further reading: Hebrews 12:1-2

So then, since we are surrounded by so great a crowd of witnesses, let us discard everything that encumbers us and the sin that clings so closely, and let us run with perseverance the race set before us, looking to Jesus, the beginning and end of our faith, who, focusing on the joy set before him, endured the cross, disregarding its shame, and has taken his seat at the right hand of the throne of God.

Suggestions for action

Ask yourself honestly if your faith is as real as it once was. Commit yourself to a more structured and disciplined devotional life. Face up to those areas where faith is weak, and seek God's help and guidance in tackling them.

Closing prayer

Living God,
    by your grace, equip, enable and enthuse us,
    so that we may faithfully walk the way of Christ,
    and finish what we started,
    to the glory of your name.
Amen.

Sixth week

The God who journeys with us

Opening prayer

Hold my hand, Lord,
  walk me through the loneliness
  and the valley of my sorrow.
Hold on to me when I'm too afraid
  to think about the future.
Let me lean on you, Lord,
  when I'm too weary to continue.
Hold my hand, Lord, through the night
  until I see the dawn.
Amen.

Author unknown

Introduction

'Come with me.' How often have we asked that of somebody? Whether it's of parents as we start a new school, a partner as we go into hospital for a consultation, or a friend as we go to a party, we value having somebody to share things with. Simply to have someone there to offer moral support, a word of encouragement, a shoulder to lean on or a helping hand can mean so much to us. As the old saying put it, 'A problem shared is a problem halved', and, in similar fashion, a joy shared is a joy doubled.

Sadly, not everyone has somebody to turn to. Many have to tackle life's challenges alone, and there are certain things that no one can share with us, not least, the experience of death. Yet as Christians we do not walk alone, for God has promised always to be with us. We may not always be conscious of that presence –

indeed, at times we may still feel very much alone – but he is by our side nonetheless, his love enfolding us, his grace renewing, his power supporting and his hand guiding. We need finally to view the journey of discipleship in this context. Though we must do all we can to ensure our progress, we are not solely dependent on our own resources. When we stumble, God is there to pick us up; when we lose our way, he is there to seek us out; when we grow weary, he is there to renew our strength; when we are unsure of the way ahead, he is there to guide. Wherever we are, whatever we face, he will be in it with us, for he does not simply call us to a journey; he also travels with us!

Activity

Quiz (see page 76).

Reading: Joshua 1:1-6, 9

Following the death of the Lord's servant Moses, the Lord spoke to Joshua son of Nun, Moses' assistant, saying, 'My servant Moses is dead. Now advance with all the people of Israel and cross the Jordan into the land that I am giving them. I will readily give to you everywhere that you set foot, as I promised to Moses. From the wilderness and the Lebanon as far as the great river, the river Euphrates, all the land of the Hittites and on towards the Great Sea in the west shall be your territory. Nobody will be able to withstand you all the days of your life. Just as I was with Moses, so I will be with you; I will not fail or forsake you. Be strong and of good courage; for you will lead this people to take possession of the land that I swore to their ancestors to give them . . . Be strong and determined, neither afraid nor anxious about anything, for the Lord your God is with you wherever you go.'

Comment

Every now and again during my time in the ministry a brochure would pop through my letterbox advertising trips to the Holy Land and encouraging me to organise a party of my own. The work involved in doing so promised to be minimal, for the practical details of ensuring comfortable hotels, good food, expert guides, and a carefully planned itinerary would all be down to the tour company. Today, with the increasingly volatile situation in the Middle East, organising such trips is a different matter; few would be willing to risk their own safety or that of others.

The contrast in those two situations may help us to appreciate something of the challenge faced by Joshua and the people of Israel as they prepared to enter and settle in the land of Canaan, the Promised Land that they had looked forward to with such anticipation for so long. For them, the journey had been anything but comfortable. They had spent 40 years wandering in the wilderness, experiencing times of hunger, doubt, exhaustion and despair; times when they must have begun to wonder if their travelling would ever be at an end. Then, what did they find? Not a land they could casually stroll into but one that was already occupied and in which they would painstakingly have to carve out a niche for themselves. To cap it all, just as they were taking all that in, they had also to come to terms with the death of their leader Moses, the one who had led them out of Egypt and throughout their testing journey thus far. For Joshua and the people of Israel, the future must have seemed daunting indeed, their initial mood of elation at nearing the end of their journey giving way to a sense of despondency and anticlimax.

Yet to those people came God's message of reassurance: 'Be strong and determined, neither afraid nor anxious about anything, for the Lord your God is with you wherever you go' (Joshua 1:9). A call to faith and courage, to go forward even though the odds seemed hopelessly stacked against them, to remember that they were not journeying alone. Whatever they might face, God tells them, he will face it with them; however great the obstacles in their path, with his help they will surmount them. If any doubted that, they needed only to remember how he had travelled with them in the wilderness, constantly assuring them of his presence and leading the way. 'The Lord went ahead of them the whole time, a pillar of cloud to guide them by day and a pillar of fire to lighten their way by night, so that they could travel whether it was light or dark. Neither the pillar of cloud by day nor the pillar of fire by night moved from its place in front of the people' (Exodus 13:21-22). The same God who had led them out of Egypt, seen them safely through the waters of the Red Sea, and walked with them during the long years in the wilderness, would continue to stand alongside them, not merely giving instructions from the sidelines but matching them step for step, a constant companion on their journey.

If that was true in the days of Moses and Joshua, how much more so is it true for us today? At the heart of the gospel stands the assurance of God's continuing presence, made clear from the very start. '"Look, the virgin shall conceive and bear a son, and they shall name him Emmanuel", which means "God is with us"' (Matthew 1:23, *NRSV*). No longer can God be seen as remote and detached; in Christ God has walked our earth, shared our humanity, and identified with us in death itself. Yet the gospel is not only about what he has done but what he continues to do, summed up in the promise of Jesus, 'I guarantee that I will be with you every day, to the very end of time' (Matthew 28:20). We see that same truth in John's Gospel, in the promise of the Holy Spirit, 'I will not leave you orphaned; I am coming to you. In a little while the world will no longer see me, but you will see me; because I live, you also will live' (John 14:18-19, *NRSV*). A guarantee to each one of us that whoever we are, wherever we go, whatever we do, he is by our side, sharing our lives, part of our daily experience. Here is the God of whom David could say: 'Even though I walk through a valley as dark as death, I fear no evil, for you are beside me, your staff and your crook are there to comfort me' (Psalm 23:4); of whom Cleopas could say, 'Were not our hearts burning within us while he was talking to us on the road' (Luke 24:32a, *NRSV*); of whom Paul could say, 'I am convinced that neither death, nor life, nor angels, nor rulers, nor things present, nor things to come, nor powers, nor height, nor depth, nor anything else in all creation, will be able to separate us from the love of God in Christ Jesus our Lord' (Romans 8:38-39, *NRSV*).

Though we turn our back on that God, he will not abandon us. Though we lose sight of him, he will still be there. Whether we step out in faith or hold back in fear, he will still be looking to lead us forward. We have only to turn to him to discover he is by our side, ready to share the journey. Our calling to walk the way of Christ demands a personal response and a lifetime's commitment. It requires careful preparation, dedication and perseverance. It involves openness to new horizons and a willingness to venture into the unknown. By ourselves, it would seem a daunting prospect, but we are not alone; we have a God who travels with us, a God who walks by our side, a God who has promised never to leave us until our journey's end.

Summary

- Not all journeys are easy. Some involve a difficult challenge.
- So it was for Joshua, charged with leading the people of Israel into the Promised Land. Having thought he had reached the end of what had already been a demanding journey, he found that there was still much to do and face.
- Impossible though the challenge must have seemed, he found inspiration in God's promise to be with his people wherever they might go. Just as he had led them out of Egypt and through the wilderness, his presence symbolised by a pillar of cloud and fire, so he would continue to lead them in the days ahead.
- For us, as Christians, that promise is all the greater. Not only has God come to us in Christ, sharing our humanity but he is also with us each day through the inner presence of his Holy Spirit. Jesus has promised to be with us always, to the end of

time. As the Apostle Paul reminds us, nothing in this life or the next will ever be able to separate us from the love of God in Christ.

- To walk the way of Christ requires faith, commitment and dedication from us, but we do not walk alone; God will be with us throughout our journey.

Discussion

- At what times have you most valued someone else's presence? In what ways did their being with you help?
- In what ways and at what times have you been most conscious of God's presence? How can we most effectively cultivate a sense of his closeness?
- Have there been times when God has seemed distant? When were these and what do you think caused them? How did you get through such times? Can you see, looking back, ways in which he *was* present though you could not see it at the time?

Prayer

Living God,
    we do not find it easy to journey in faith.
We want a clearer idea of what the future holds,
    a knowledge of where we are heading
    and how we are going to get there.
Yet we know that neither life nor faith is like that,
    few things as definite as we would like them to be.
Inspire us, though, by the knowledge
    that you are journeying with us
    every step of the way.
May that truth equip us with courage to step out into the unknown,
    with faith to follow wherever you lead,

with trust to walk with humility
and with commitment to travel on to our journey's end.
Through Jesus Christ our Lord.
Amen.

Meditation of Joshua

Be strong, he said,
   be very courageous,
   and I will be with you wherever you go.
It was a wonderful promise,
   an unchanging hope in an uncertain world,
   and I needed that then, more than I can tell you.
For suddenly I was on my own, or that's how it seemed;
   our leader taken from us,
   man of God,
   man of the people,
   man we would see no more.
He'd be a hard act to follow, we'd realised that from the beginning,
   each of us dreading the day when the end must finally come,
   but when it did I never dreamt for a moment
   I'd be the one they'd turn to,
   the one approved by Moses himself.
I felt lost,
   bewildered –
   we all did –
   a ship without a rudder,
   an ox without a yoke.
For he'd always been there, as long as we could remember,
   leading us safely on through thick and thin.
And we'd made it, so we thought,
   our destination reaching out to greet us,
   land flowing with milk and honey,
   peace, prosperity, at last.
Only it wasn't,

for though the journey was over, the conquest had just begun,
and I was petrified,
overwhelmed by the scale of the challenge,
awed by the responsibility.
Who was I to take it on? –
nothing special,
no one gifted,
a plain ordinary man
with a quite extraordinary mission.
I couldn't have done it,
not alone,
no way.
But I didn't have to, of course,
for God was with us as he promised,
every step of the way;
there to challenge,
there to guide,
there to bless.
When my spirit failed, he was with me,
when my foot slipped he picked me up,
always helping,
always leading,
a never-failing stream of love.
He asked one thing, that's all,
and it wasn't much,
hard though we found it,
often though we failed.
It was to stay true to the commandments he had given,
the book of the law,
holding them fast in our minds,
meditating on them day and night –
never swerving,
never turning,
but walking in faith, come what may.
We had our moments, like I say,
still do, sadly –

even now some people looking back with regret
and ahead with consternation.
Well, it's up to them, I've done my bit –
it's their choice, no one else's –
but as for me and my family,
there's no question,
no doubt in our minds:
we will serve the Lord.

Further reading: Leviticus 26:12

I will walk among you, and be your God, and you shall be my
people.

Suggestions for action

Whatever situation you find yourself in, remind yourself that God
is with you in it. Share it with him.

Closing prayer

Loving God,
    teach us to walk with you,
    confident that though we do not know the way,
    you will guide our footsteps
    and travel with us
    to our journey's end.
Through Jesus Christ our Lord.
Amen.

Appendix 1

Activities

First week: Called to a journey

Journeys quiz

1. Who starred between 1940 and 1952 in the highly successful series of *Road to . . .* comedies?
2. Who wrote *Gulliver's Travels*?
3. Who wrote *Around the World in Eighty Days* and *Journey to the Centre of the Earth*?
4. Who sang *The Road to Nowhere*?
5. Who wrote *A Passage to India* and *The Longest Journey*?
6. Who wrote *Travels With My Aunt*?
7. Who wrote about time travel in the classic novel *The Time Machine*?
8. To whom is the Greek epic poem *The Odyssey* ascribed?
9. Which British travel writer wrote *Journey Across Britain*?
10. Who wrote *The Hitchhiker's Guide to the Galaxy*?

After the quiz, invite participants to talk briefly together about their sense of calling, and about what they believe is involved in following Jesus.

Second week: A personal journey

Personal journeys quiz

1. Which Lancastrian, born in Blackburn in 1907, is almost synonymous with the Lake District for his many books and sketches of the area?

2. Which American novelist and writer of over 50 travel books first rose to public prominence through his books *The Great Railway Bazaar* and *The Old Patagonian Express*?

3. Who wrote the book *Saved* concerning his astonishing survival in the Southern Ocean following the capsize of his yacht in a round-the-world yachting race?

4. Which Carthaginian general is famed for the journey he undertook to outwit the Romans during the Second Punic Wars?

5. Which balloonist had a narrow escape attempting the first solo balloon flight around the world, and what is the name of his rival who has made several abortive attempts to beat him to the record?

6. Which bespectacled TV broadcaster and journalist became famous for his wry humour in a long-running documentary series exploring countries and people across the world?

7. Which celebrated sportsman has regularly taken part in marathon walks to raise money for leukaemia research?

8. Who travelled across the world as the original presenter of the television series *Wish You Were Here*?

9. Which American travel writer wrote about his travels in Britain under the title *Notes From a Small Island*?

10. Which popular travel writer was once a member of the Monty Python team?

After finishing the quiz, invite people to share what following Jesus means to them.

Third week: Equipped for the journey

Choices

You are sent on a four-month hiking expedition, for which you are allowed to take three luxury items (i.e. other than vital equipment). What will you take and why?

Allow time for group members to decide on their three choices (be ready with pen and paper, in case anyone should want to write these down), and then invite people to share these with other members of the group. Allow informal discussion to develop concerning the things we consider most important in life.

Fourth week: A Journey of Discovery

Explorers quiz

How well do you know your history of explorers? Identify the following from the clues given.

1. His name is particularly associated with the area of Labrador, Newfoundland and New England.
2. One of the most famed explorers of all, due to his journey in the *Santa Maria* to San Salvador, Cuba and Hispaniola.
3. Scottish missionary whose name has been immortalised as a celebrated explorer of Africa.
4. Yorkshireman, captain of the *Endeavour*, who explored the South Pacific, including New Zealand and Antarctica.
5. Elizabethan explorer reckoned to be the first Englishman to circumnavigate the globe.
6. Irish explorer whose name, alongside that of Captain Scott, is associated with Antarctica and the South Pole.
7. Portuguese explorer, reckoned to be the first European to reach India by the sea route.
8. Polar explorer, celebrated as the first man to reach the South Pole.
9. A medieval traveller and explorer famed for his accounts of experiences in China.
10. Anthropologist and explorer whose name is forever associated with the balsawood raft *Kon Tiki*.

After completing the quiz, talk briefly together about the qualities and characteristics needed to be an explorer. Consider how far these may relate to Christian discipleship.

Fifth week: Completing the journey

Pop quiz

This activity can either be conducted as a straight quiz, or, if you have a recording of the song in question, you can ask if anyone in the group can identify the song and singer/s.

Name the group or singer who had a hit with the following songs.

1. The long and winding road
2. Davy's on the road again
3. Goodbye Yellow Brick Road
4. Walking back to happiness.
5. Walk on by
6. You'll never walk alone
7. Keep on running
8. These boots are made for walking
9. I'm walking in the air
10. The walk of life

After finishing the quiz, discuss the sort of things that are necessary to complete any major journey. Explore how we might relate these to faith.

Sixth week: The God who journeys with us

Quiz

Complete the following grid from the cryptic clues supplied. All of the answers are those who in some way stick close to people, travelling with them wherever they go.

1.	_ _ _ _ _ **G** _ _ _ _
2.	_ **O** _ _ _ _ _ _ _
3.	_ _ _ **D** _ _
4.	_ _ **I** _ _
5.	_ **S** _ _ _ _
6.	_ _ _ _ _ **W**
7.	_ **I** _ _
8.	_ **T** _ _ _ _ _
9.	_ **H** _ _ _ _ _ _ _
10.	_ **U** _ _ _ _ _ _ _ _ _ _ _
11.	_ _ _ _ _ _ **S** _ _ _ _ _ _

1. Long-limbed protector? (4, 5)
2. Patrols the graveyard, perhaps? (9)
3. Helps you to think before the Queen comes (6)
4. Uniformed young lady leading you on, perhaps? (5)
5. Shows you to your car perhaps? (6)
6. A private detective with a sunny disposition? (6)
7. PA comes to your rescue? (4)
8. Someone who follows too closely for comfort (7)
9. A Victorian woman could hardly do without one (9)
10. A little help from above? (8, 5)
11. Canonised supporter of gypsies? (2, 11)

After completing the quiz, briefly discuss which of the answers might be applied to God, and why.

Appendix 2

Answers

First week

1. Bob Hope, Bing Crosby and Dorothy Lamour
2. Jonathan Swift
3. Jules Verne
4. Talking Heads
5. E. M. Forster
6. Graham Greene
7. H. G. Wells
8. Homer
9. John Hillaby
10. Douglas Adams

Second week

1. Alfred Wainwright
2. Paul Theroux
3. Tony Bullimore
4. Hannibal
5. Richard Branson and Steve Fossett
6. Sir Alan Whicker
7. Ian Botham
8. Judith Chalmers
9. Bill Bryson
10. Michael Palin

Fourth week

1. John Cabot
2. Christopher Columbus
3. David Livingstone
4. Captain (James) Cook
5. Sir Francis Drake
6. Sir Ernest Henry Shackleton
7. Vasco da Gama
8. Roald Amundsen
9. Marco Polo
10. Thor Heyerdahl

Fifth week

1. The Beatles
2. Manfred Mann and his Earthband
3. Elton John
4. Helen Shapiro
5. Dionne Warwick
6. Gerry and the Pacemakers
7. Spencer Davis Group
8. Nancy Sinatra
9. Aled Jones
10. Dire Straits

Sixth week

1. ARMED GUARD
2.   BODYGUARD
3.   MINDER
4.   GUIDE
5.   ESCORT
6. SHADOW
7.   AIDE
8.   STALKER
9.   CHAPERONE
10.   GUARDIAN ANGEL
11. ST CHRISTOPHER

Also in this series:
Living with questions – exploring faith and doubt
Paul – the man and the mission
Something to share – communicating the good news
Prayer – the fundamental questions
Unsung gifts – the Spirit at work in the New Testament
Love – the key to it all
Women of faith – what they teach us

Also by Nick Fawcett:
No ordinary man (books 1 and 2)
Resources for reflective worship on the person of Jesus

The unfolding story
Resources for reflective worship on the Old Testament

Grappling with God (books 1-4)
Old Testament studies for personal and small-group use

To put it another way
Resources for reflective worship on the Parables

Are you listening?
Honest prayers about life

Prayers for all seasons (books 1 and 2)
A comprehensive resource for public worship

Getting it across
One hundred talks for family worship

Decisions, decisions
A Lent study course

Promises, promises
An Advent study course

Daily prayer
A book of daily devotions

All the above titles are available from your local Christian bookshop
or direct from Kevin Mayhew Ltd, telephone 01449 737978,
fax: 01449 737834, email: sales@kevinmayhewltd.com